NATIONAL GEOGRAPHIC

Count the Animals

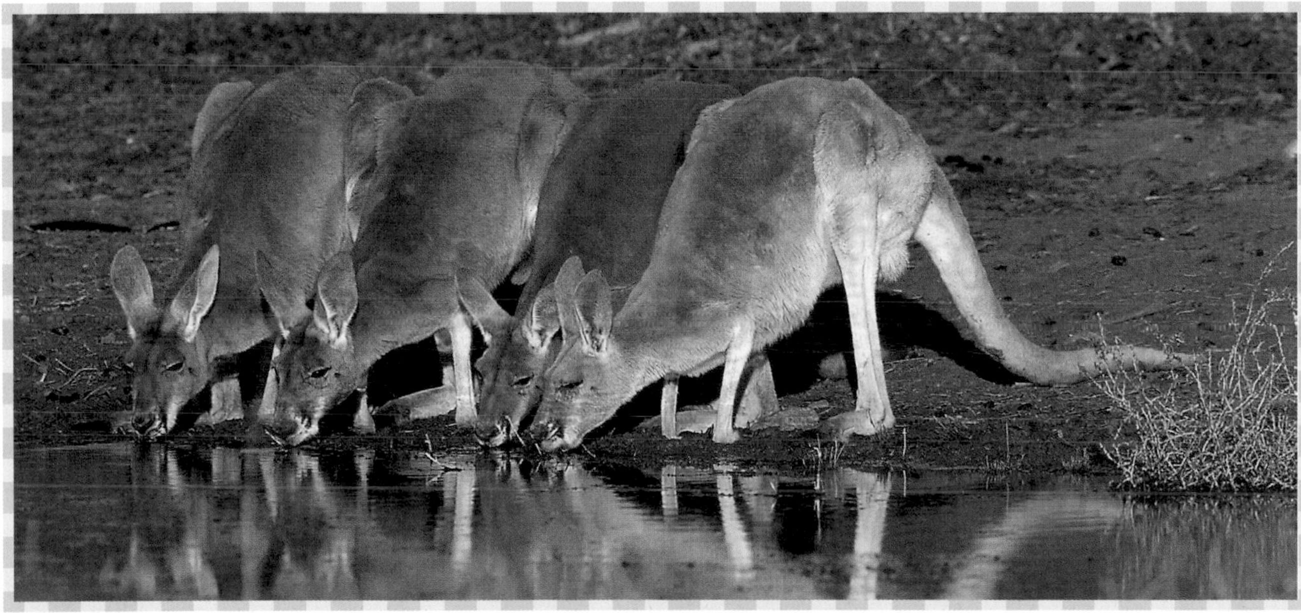

Terry O'Brady

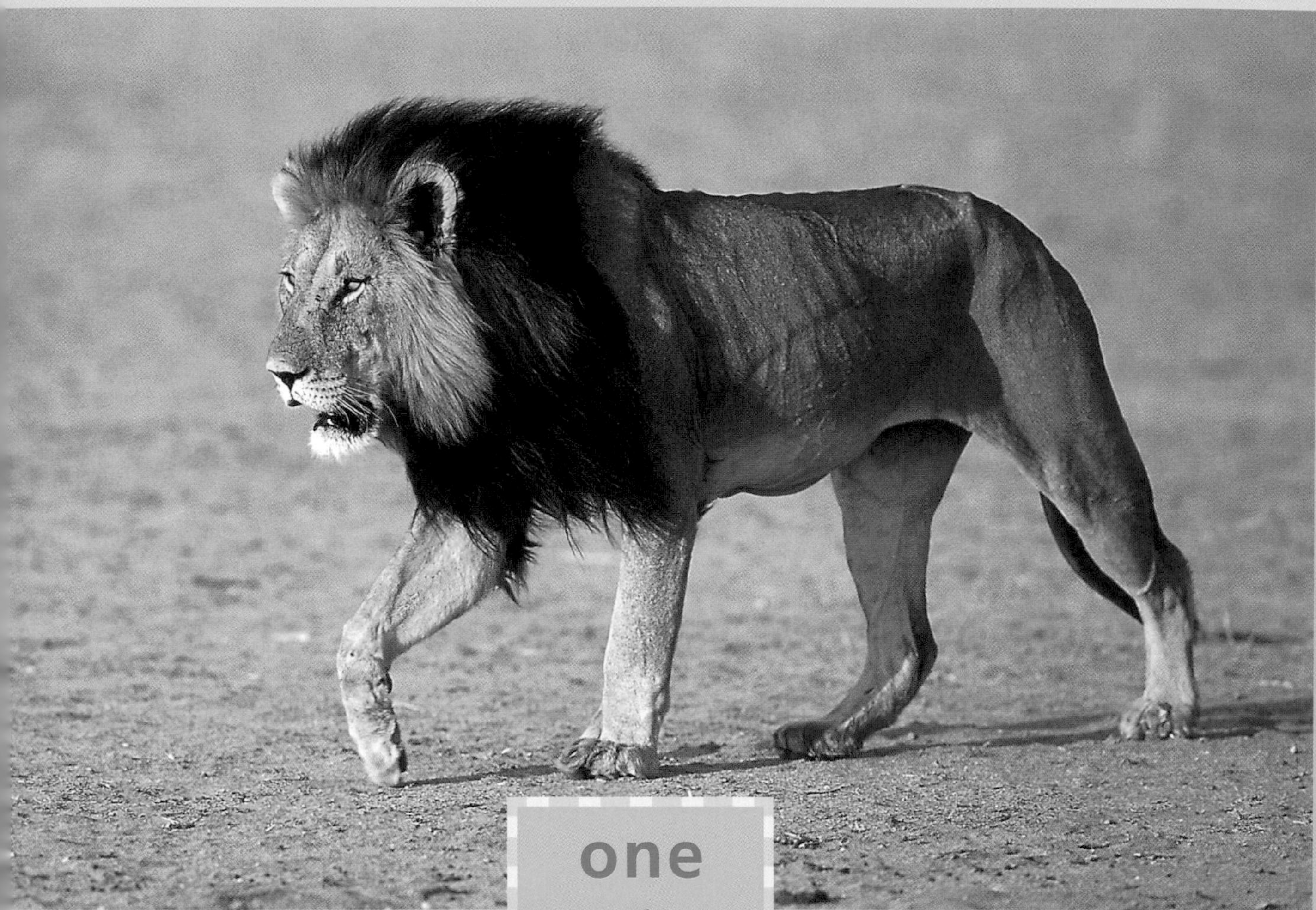

one

1

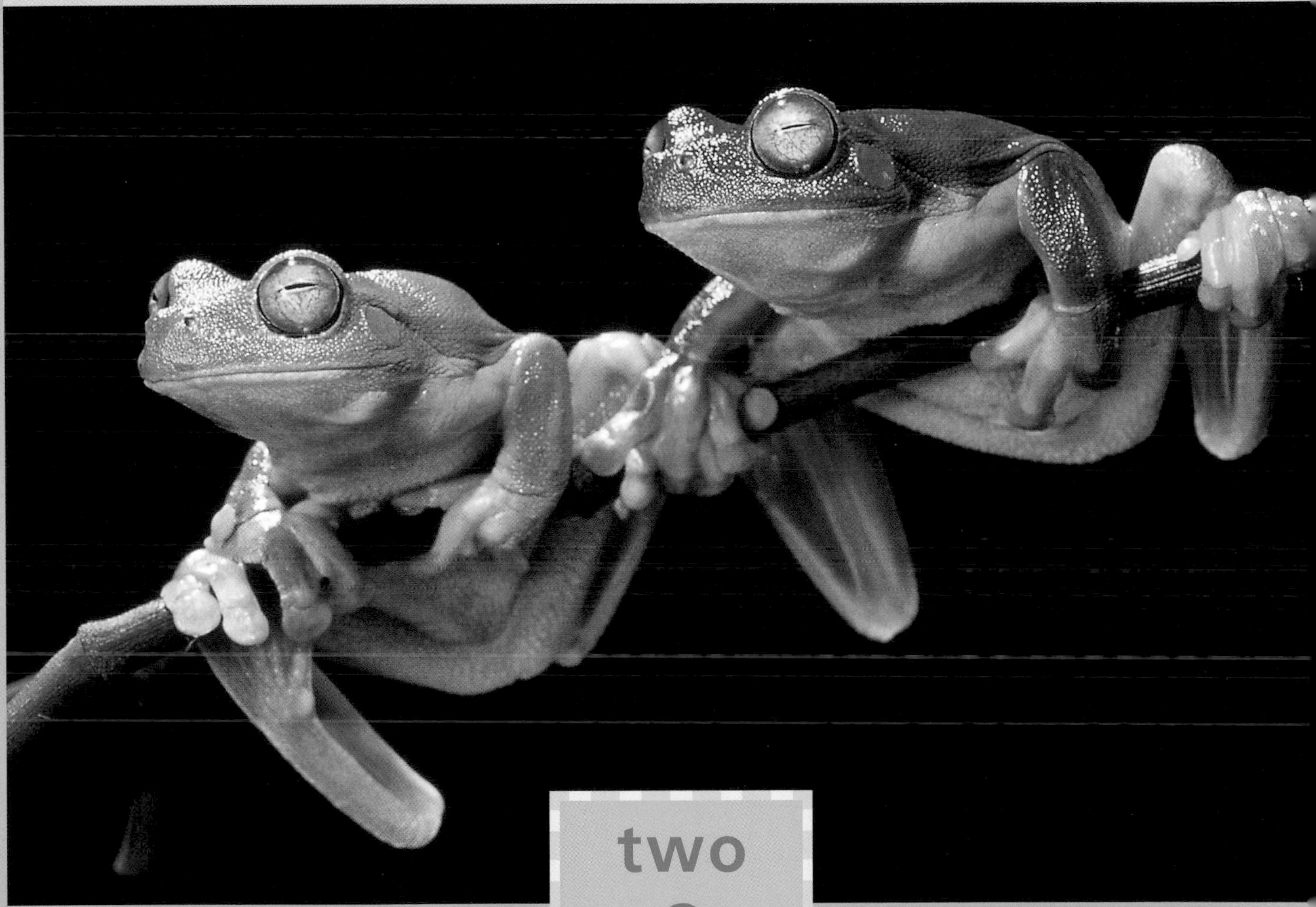

two
2

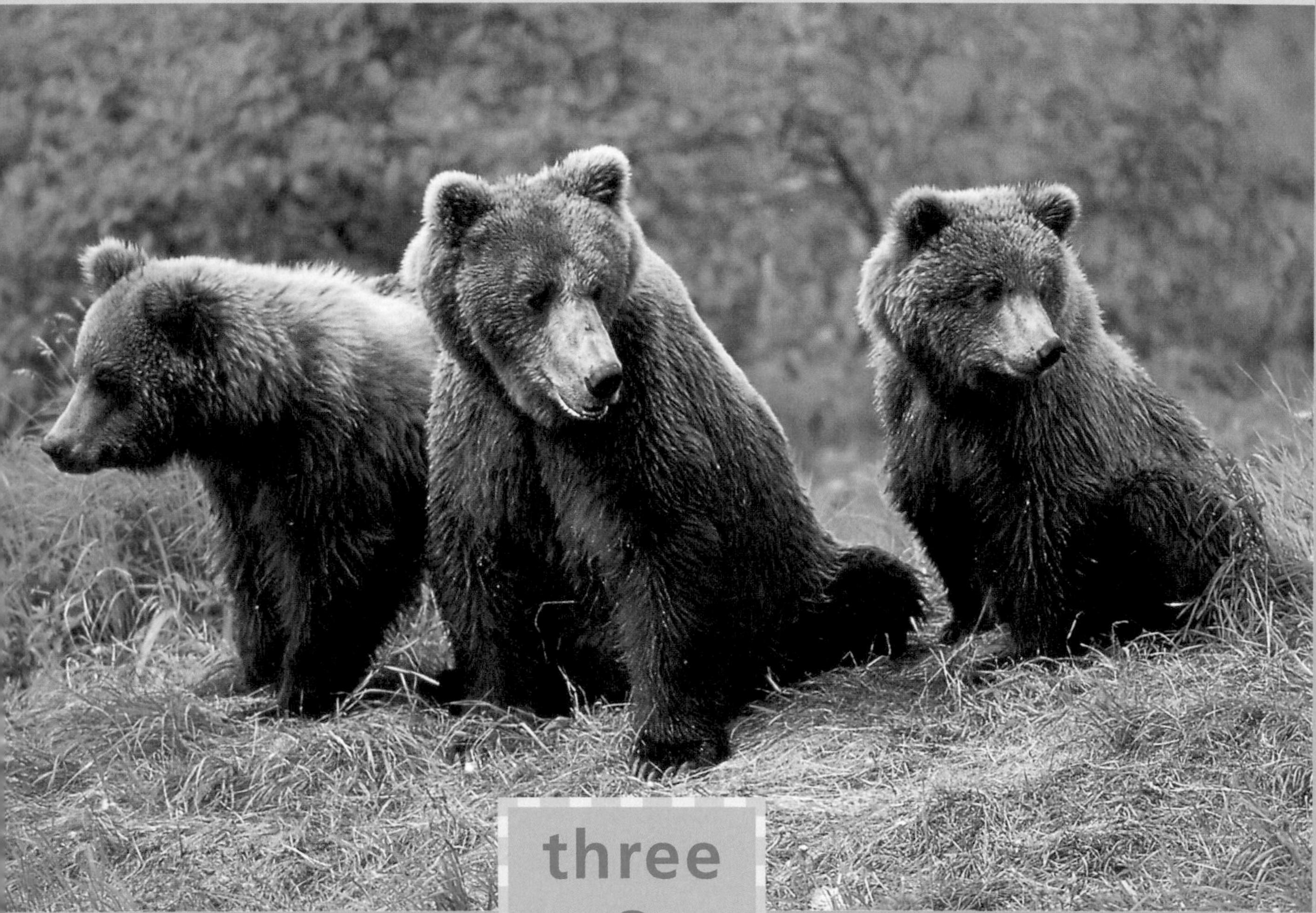

three

3

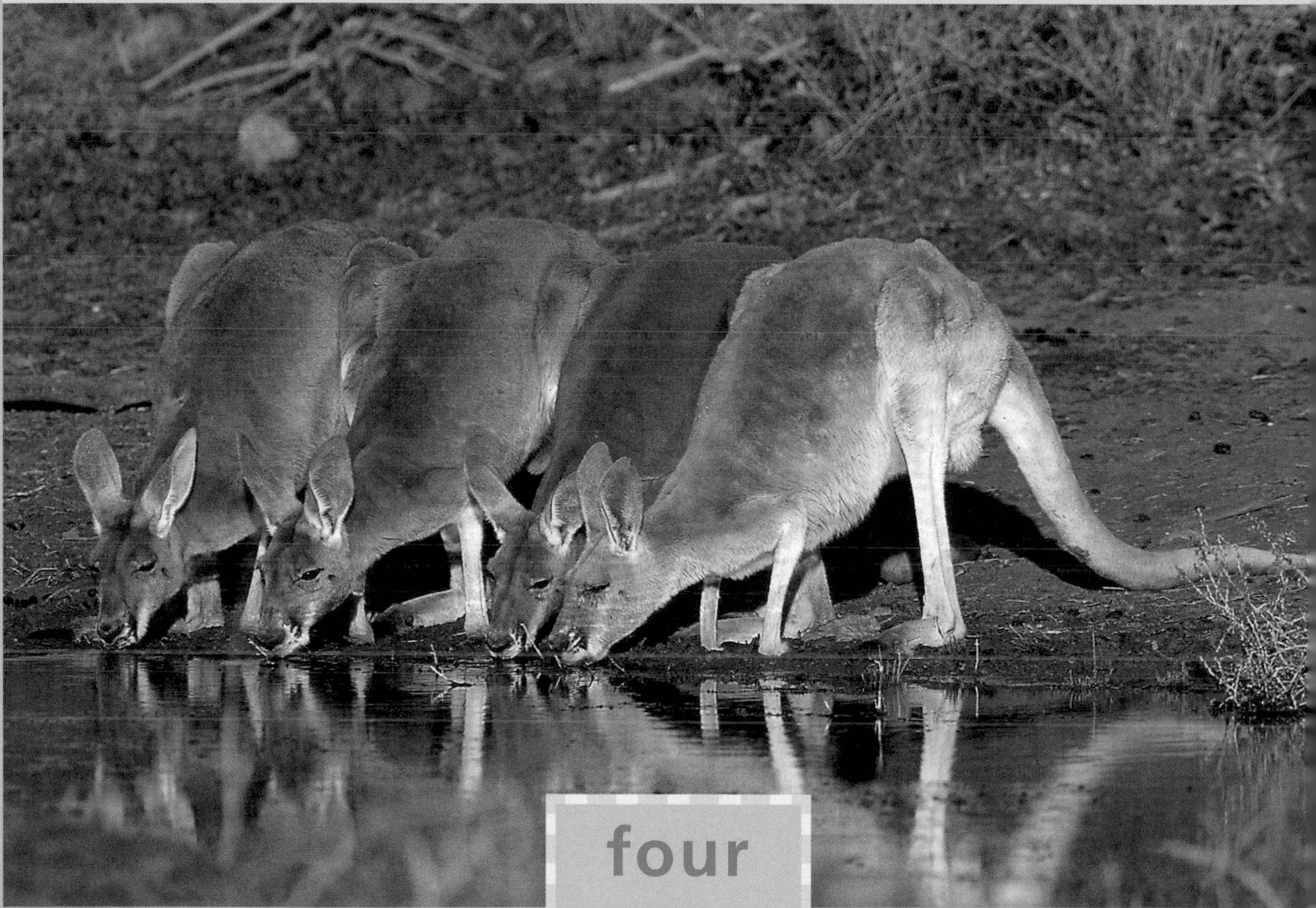

four

4

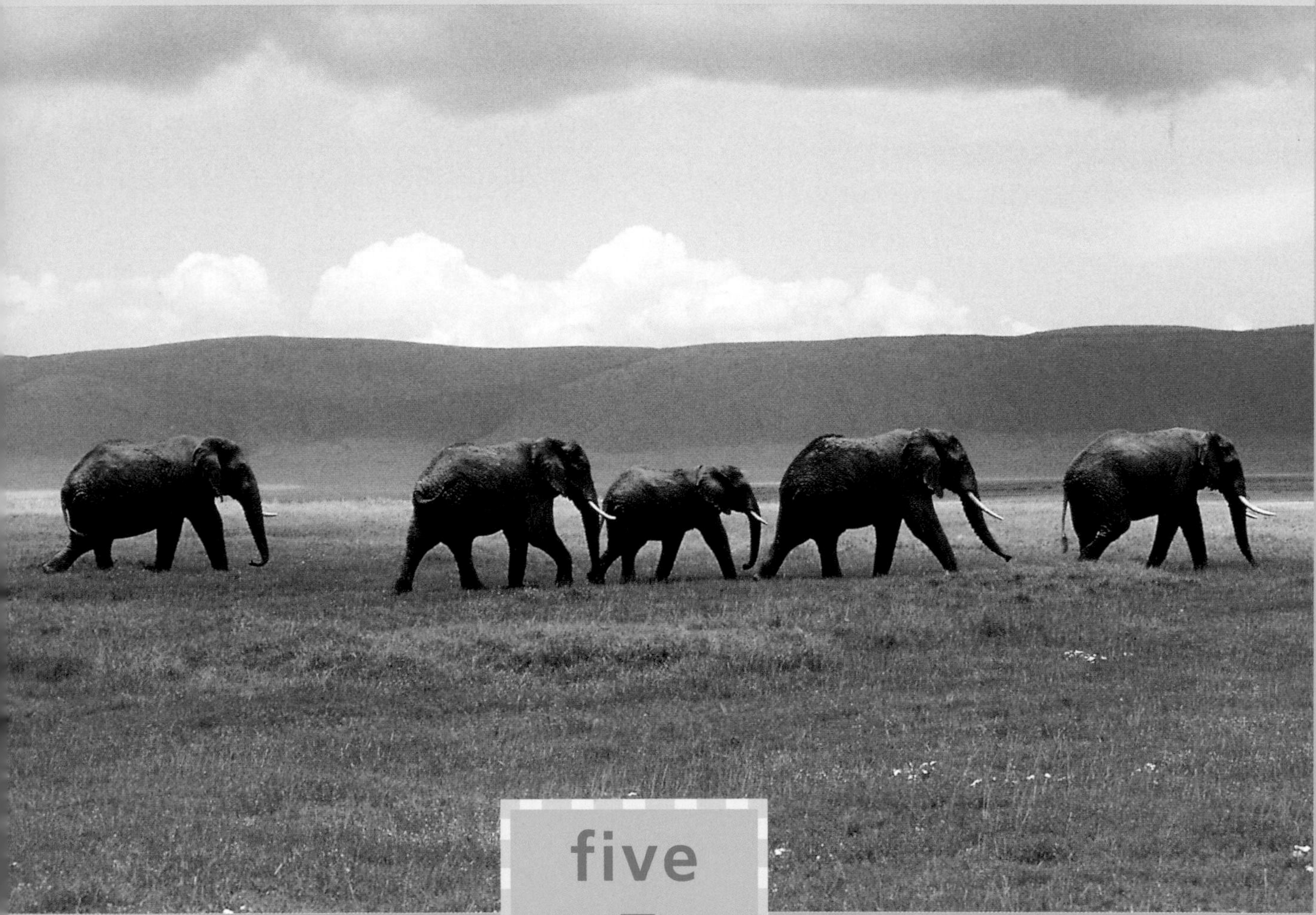

five

5

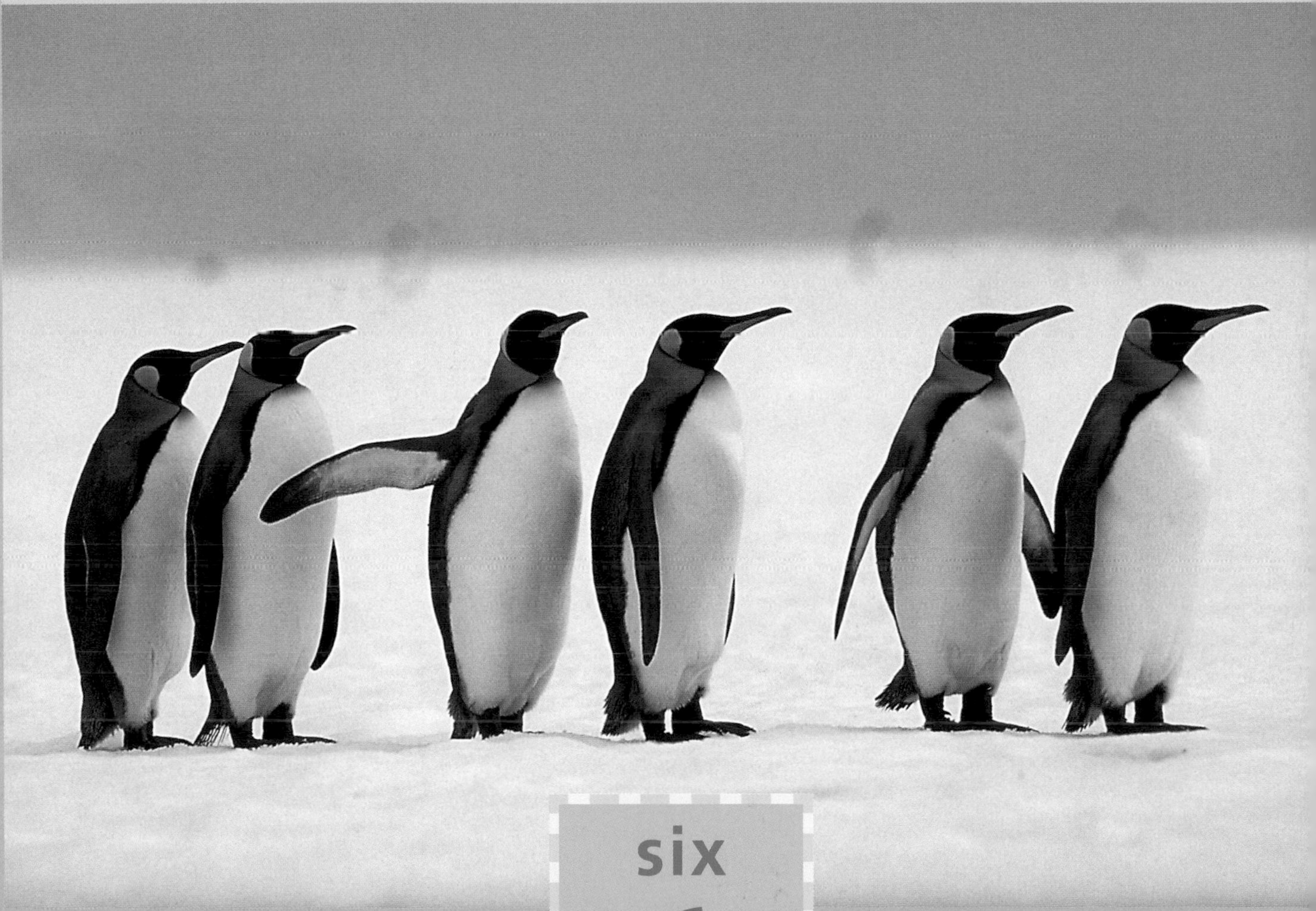

six

6

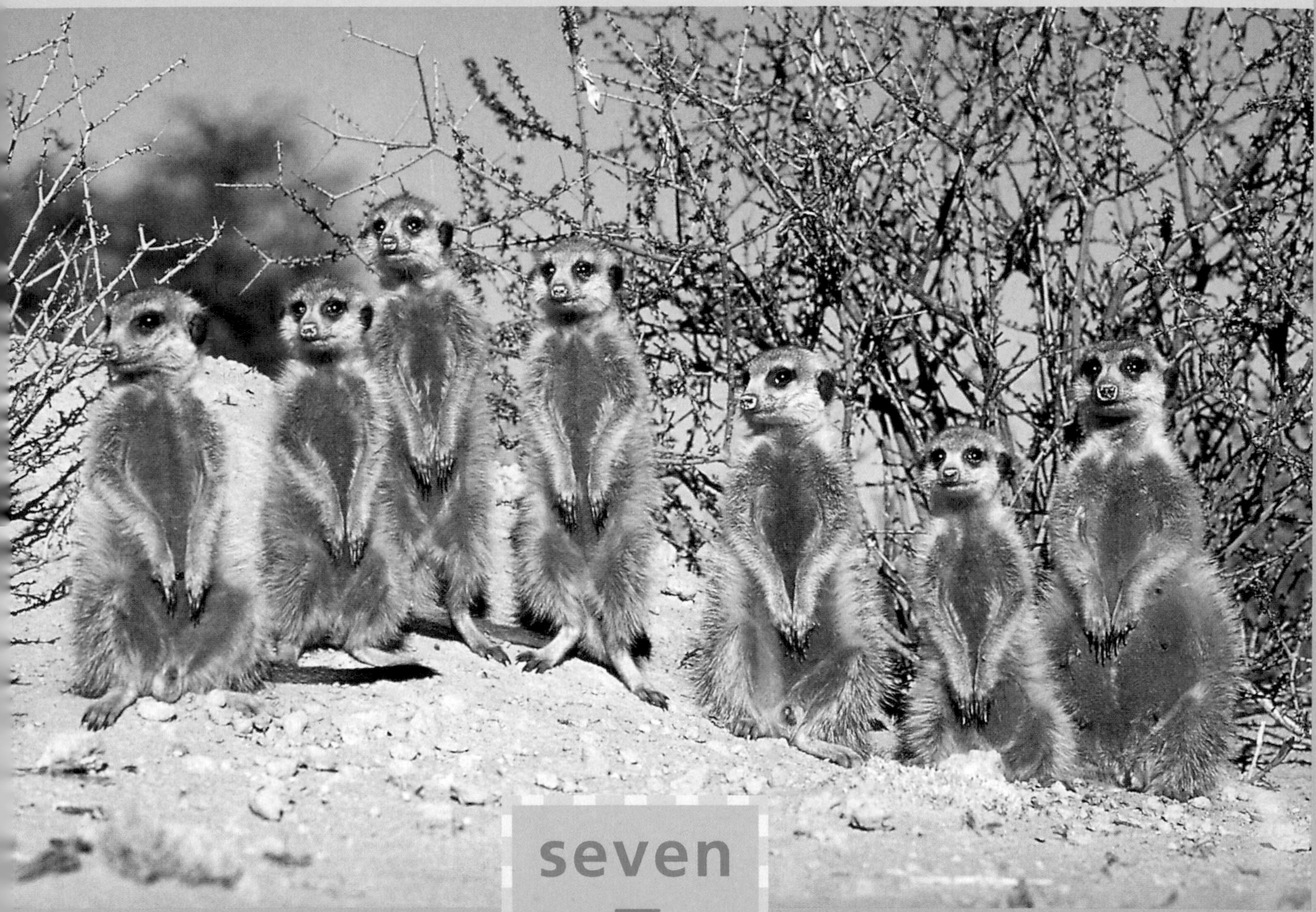

seven

7

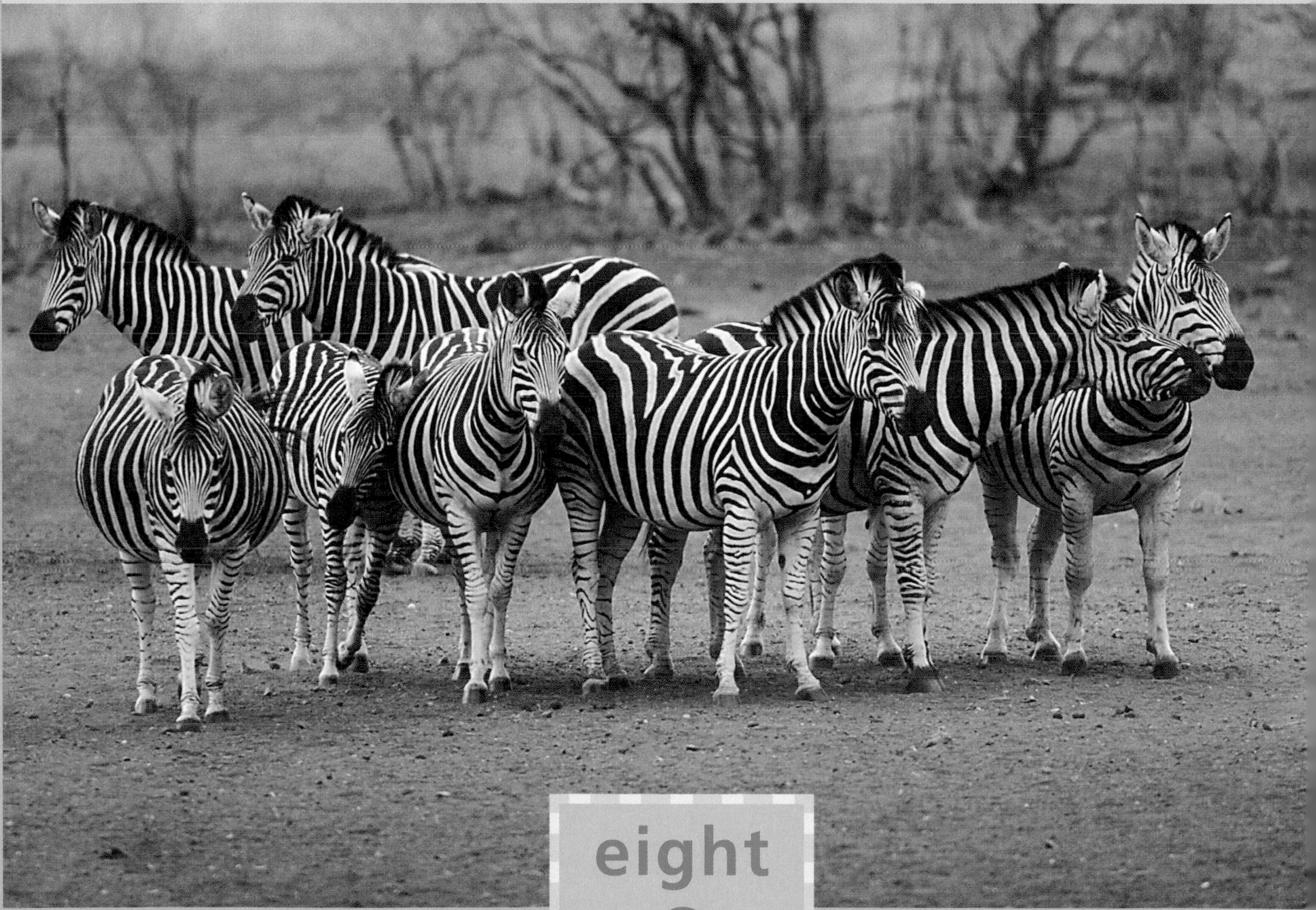

eight

8

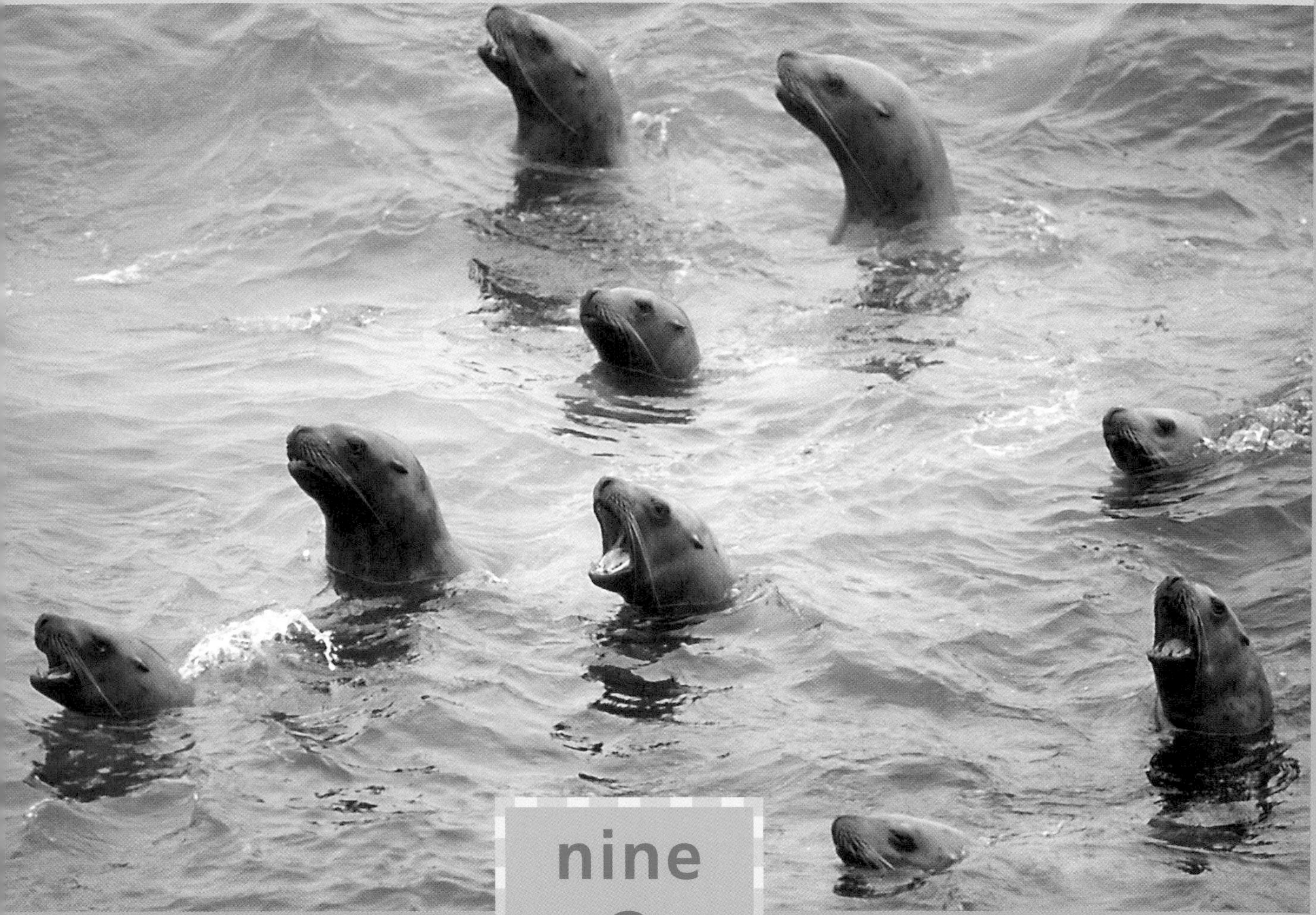

nine
9

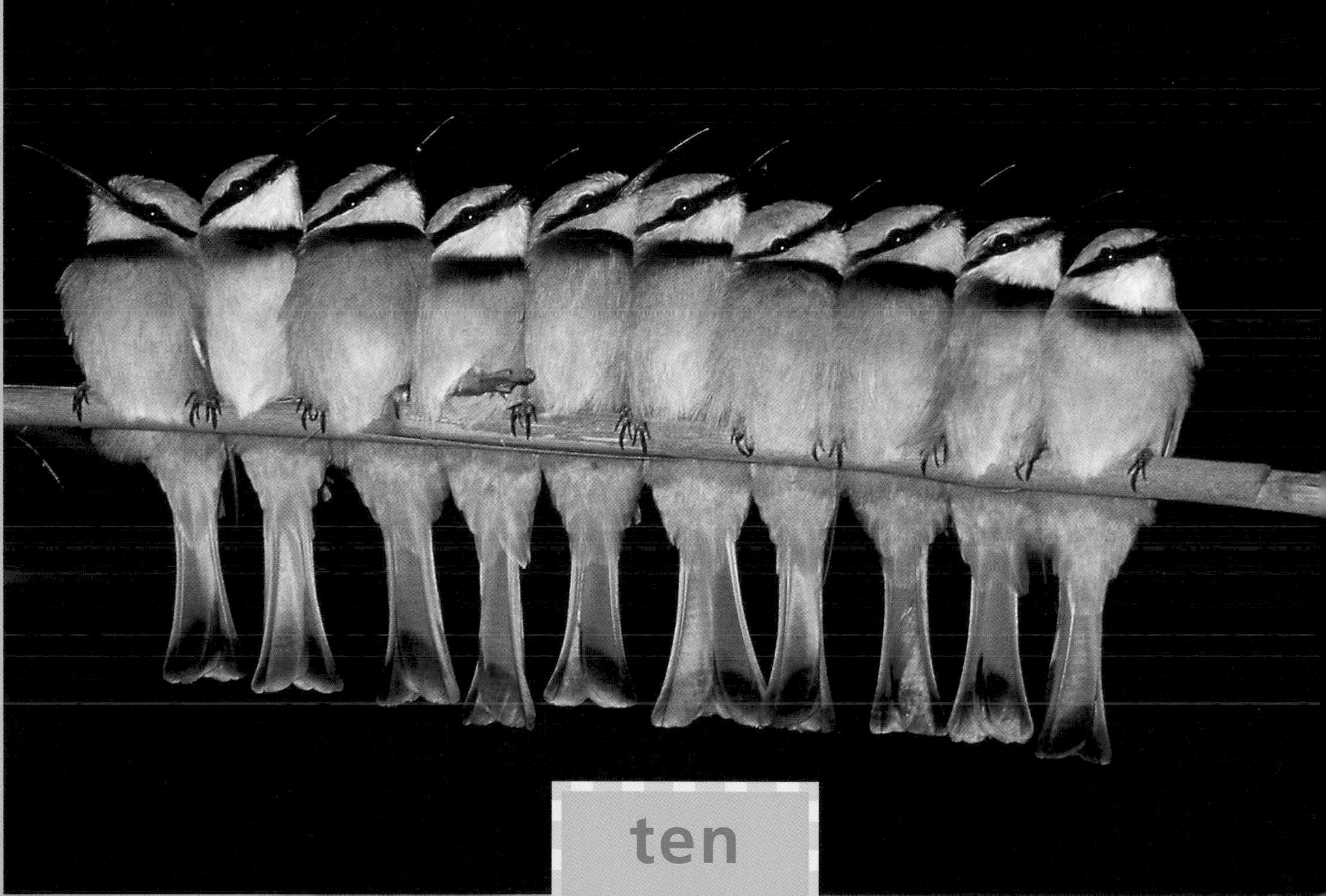

ten

10

one 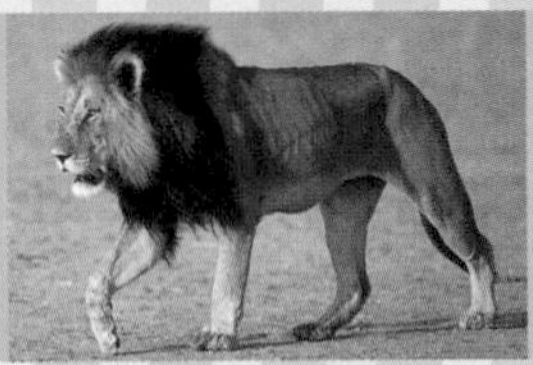 1

two 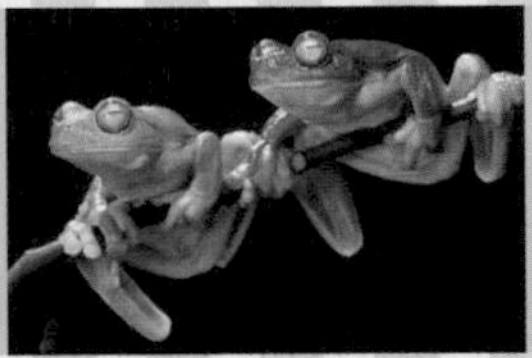 2

three 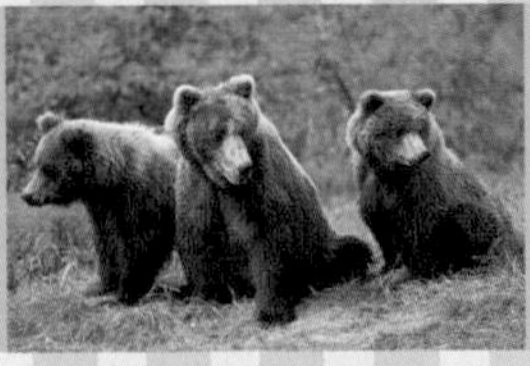 3

four 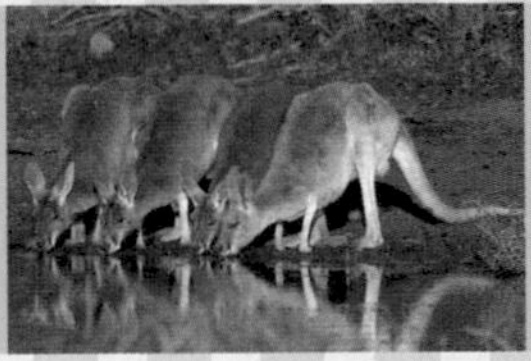 4

five 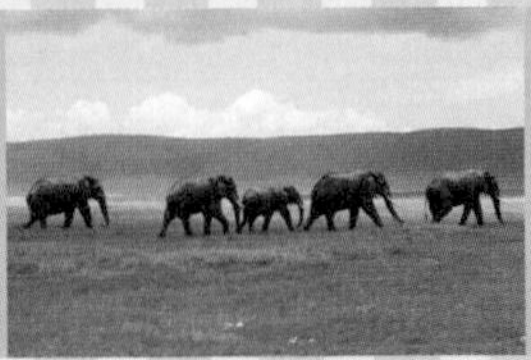 5

six 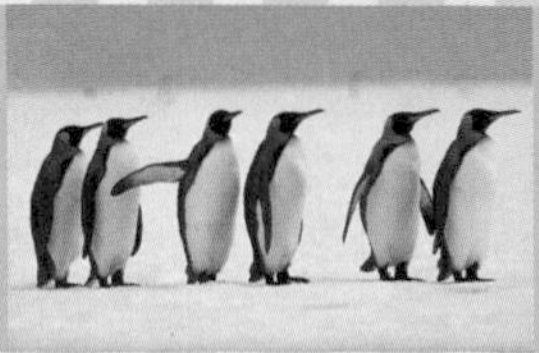 6

seven 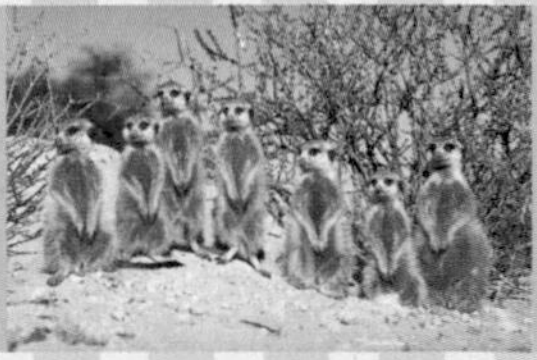 7

eight 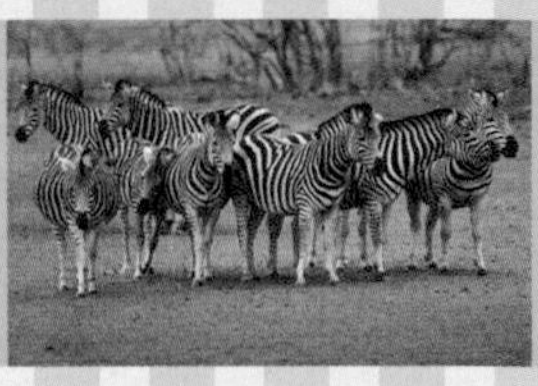 8

nine 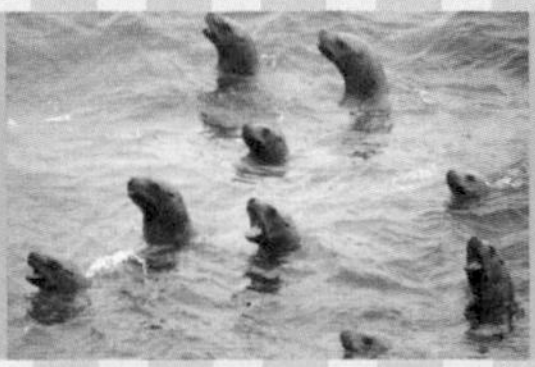 9

ten 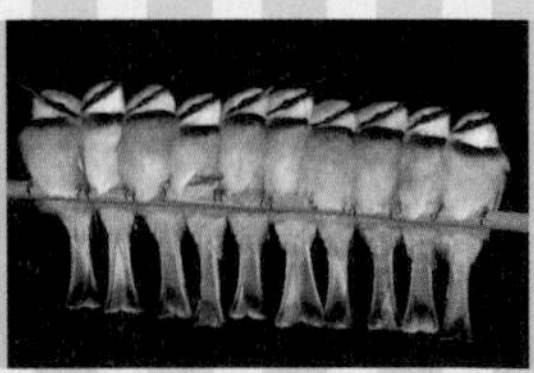 10